How To
GET MORE
New Customers,
Clients And Patients
With Direct Mail

VICTOR URBINA

Published by Urbina Media Group
3001 E Paisano Dr, El Paso, TX 79905, U.S.A.

How To Get More New Customers, Clients And Patients With Direct Mail - 1st ed.

ISBN-10: 0692675094
ISBN-13: 978-0692675090
LCCN: 2016904911

Printed in the United States of America

DEDICATION
DEDICACIÓN

To my wife and parents.
To all the entrepreneurs of the world
who get up EVERY morning
<u>ready and willing</u>
to run ANOTHER marathon.

A mi esposa y mis padres.
A todos los emprendedores del mundo
que despiertan CADA mañana
<u>*listos y dispuestos*</u>
a correr OTRO maratón.

TABLE OF CONTENTS

ACKNOWLEDGMENTS

I would like to acknowledge Dean Jackson as the originator of the idea to write this book.

Thanks a million Dean,
more cheese, less whiskers!

i

Introduction

*"Our business is infested
with idiots who try to impress
by using pretentious jargon."*
— David Ogilvy

The purpose of this book is very simple. To help you get more new customers, clients and patients for your business or professional practice using direct mail.

Yes, you read that correctly direct mail. Not email or Facebook or any other shiny new tech gadget that promises to deliver customers in droves, but remains largely unproven. This is about hardcore direct mail.

In this book I'll be answering some of your most burning questions about direct mail such as. What is it? What types of direct mail can I use? What are the guidelines I have to follow? And how do I determine if my direct mail campaign was a winner?

I'm even going to throw in some case studies at the end of the book of people in different industries who are successfully using direct mail. Why am I doing that? So that you don't put down the book and say, "Those are all good ideas, but they would never work in my business, my business is different." Because honestly your business is not different. And there's no business or professional practice in the world that direct mail couldn't help.

I've been using direct mail for over six years. And I learned how to use it out of desperation and made just about every single mistake you can make along the way. Here's my story.

I own UPS Stores all over the United States. I've been a UPS store franchisee for over 10 years. Needless to say I've had my ups and downs. I've opened new stores and I've had to close unsuccessful stores.

For the first few years I was in business, I was crushing it; business was more than I could handle at times, and life was good. I thought I was the Steve Jobs of UPS stores.

So what does one do when they think they have it all figured out? They expand. And expand I did, but maybe a little too much. What I didn't realize was that the reason my first store was so successful was that I had a phenomenal location. I had no competition and, thus, had no need to market; buyers were all mine.

After I expanded, I realized that I wasn't the only game in town and that I had to start marketing my stores. If you're as successful early in your career as I was, chances are, you don't take the time to learn or sharpen your skills. Instead, I started "marketing" my stores—I use that word liberally because, looking back, all I was really doing was throwing away tons of cash.

Then one January, I realized I had about six months of money left in the bank before I would be out of business. It was the wake-up call all business owners hate getting. I had to completely change the way I did business. I had to learn how to effectively and profitably market my stores.

After two years of intense study, frenetic implementation, and countless sleepless nights, I was able to put my stores in a secure financial position. Today, we have had continued growth for four straight years.

I still made my fair share of marketing mistakes, which were a welcome outcome because they allowed me to correct my course, but I've had far more verifiable wins than losses in my marketing efforts.

Direct mail was one of the tools I gravitated towards early on in my turn around and has been one of the most reliable tools in my arsenal. In hindsight, it took me about two years of failure to figure out how to use direct mail effectively, so by reading this book you're going to essentially leap frog years of learning and learn from all of my mistakes.

Sound good?

So back to why I wrote this book. I wrote this book because I see a huge gap in the marketing landscape. It seems that everyone is touting search engine optimization (SEO), Facebook, email marketing and the dreaded B word... branding! Don't get me wrong, I think that these are key components of an effective marketing strategy, but to rely solely upon them is a huge mistake. For example, Facebook recently changed its ad policies to shut down many successful marketing campaigns, and Google is constantly changing its algorithms, making SEO reliant on the whims of techno geeks comfortably employed and not fighting for a dollar the way you and I are.

There is a breadth of opportunity for a business or professional practice that stands apart by embracing direct mail.

Consider this fact: Google, the king of online marketing, is one of the top 10 direct mailers year after year. They use direct mail postcards and letters to drive businesses online to sign up for their AdWords platform. If you take a moment to examine what's happening to your mailbox every year you'll realize that it is probably getting less and less crowded. On the other hand what's happening to your inbox and the internet? Advertising overload. Convinced yet?

Let me bottom line it for you. I come from a world where I have to fight it out tooth and nail with FedEx, the U.S. Postal Service (USPS), and sometimes-even UPS itself. A world where customers begrudgingly come to my stores because they have to, not because they want to.

On top of that, I rely on employees that have an associate degree—at best—to wait on my customers and deliver phenomenal service, all for an average sale between $20-$30.

In spite of this, I still went from one store to multiple stores in less than seven years in one of the most competitive marketplaces AND a recession.

If you, on the other hand, have a business or professional practice that is even the tiniest bit sexier than a UPS store, then I think you're going to do fantastic. If your average ticket is in the hundreds or thousands, then you're going to do just fine. AND if you have a "want to" business or practice where people happily walk in your door and give you money, then again you're going to do just fine.

You see, I view marketing a business as a science. It begins with a hypothesis (a marketing idea) that you want to prove true (make money with), so you set up an experiment (direct mail campaign) to test it. As your experiment unfolds, you start collecting data (revenue) that you then analyze to see if your hypothesis was proven or not (what was the return on your investment).

If you collected good data, then you rerun the experiment altering a variable to test how the data changes. You repeat this process until you have optimum predictable results from your direct mail campaign.

What I'm going to share with you is not new. I didn't invent direct mail or even pioneer it. I'm merely a user who's gotten REALLY good at it. I've had a lot of help along the way. I've invested heavily in developing my skills and have hired professionals to handle the direct mail components that I didn't know enough about, didn't want to do or simply didn't have time to do.

At times these investments seemed steep, but the financial return on them was immeasurable. I made the decision early on that I wasn't going to be "penny wise and dollar foolish." I surrounded myself with a team of trusted advisors to help me along the way.

The biggest discovery I made from doing this was that my greatest breakthroughs always came from people who were outside my industry, people whose opinions I would've dismissed in the early days when things were going great because I thought they couldn't possibly understand my business. Boy was I wrong.

My business really took off once I started working with outsiders. Picking their brains about the latest killer direct mail campaign they were using then modifying it to use with my stores. I couldn't explain why, but it just worked. Sometimes that's all you need... for it to just work.

Having said that, please keep an open mind as you read this. I know it can be hard at times, but hey you didn't get into entrepreneurship because it was easy right? I want thank you profusely for investing not only your hard earned money, but your time in this book. I wish you happy reading!

1

WHAT IS DIRECT MAIL?

What is direct mail? That's an excellent question. The answer is very complex because direct mail is a very misunderstood tool of marketing. A better question though is, "How can I use direct mail to get more new customers, clients and patients to my business or practice?" But we'll get to that shortly.

The Merriam-Webster dictionary defines it as, "Printed matter prepared for soliciting business or contributions and mailed directly to individuals." In layman's terms it's information on a postcard, letter, oversized postcard or a piece of lump email that you mail in order to attract customers, clients or patients to your business or practice.

The USPS website defines direct mail, or bulk mail as they call it, as, "Large quantities of mail prepared for mailing at reduced postage." So what exactly do they mean by "reduced postage"? Well, bulk prices are lower than single piece prices, and single piece means that you're paying the full postage price, kinda like putting a forever stamp on your postcard or letter.

So why does the Postal Service offer bulk pricing? The Postal Service offers lower pricing for bulk mailing because you're going to be doing about half the work that otherwise they would have had to do. For example, presorting the mail by 3 or 5-digit ZIP code or transporting the mail to a destination post office. The point is that they're giving you a discount because you're doing the work for them, leaving them only the home delivery portion.

So at this point, you're probably wondering, "How do I get these discounts?" Well, in order to get them there's a couple of things you'll need to do before you even get your first postcard or letter printed. First off, you need to get a mailing permit directly from your nearest business mail entry unit. This is basically the post office giving you permission to mail in bulk. Next, after you fill out the permit and file it you'll need to pay an annual mailing fee. The permission does come at a price, but the fee is really nominal. Additionally, if you're going to be using a mailing indicia, which I recommend you apply for even if you don't use it 100% of the time, instead of pre-cancelled stamps there's a second form and one-time fee you're going to have to file and pay. Again getting these discounts on mailing does require an upfront investment, if you're not going to be mailing a lot you might want to reconsider an indicia. Finally, you're going to have to set up a payment account with the Postal Service that will be debited every time you present a mailing. But let's shift gears for a second, let me tell you why. I wanna talk a bit of strategy.

A lot of businesses think that direct mail should be used to send 10,000 postcards all at once and then pray for the best. We'll hope has never been a good marketing strategy and if that's the underlying strategy you use when you invest in direct mail then, unfortunately, you're not going to get very far. More than likely you're going to write off direct mail as a viable source to generate more new customers, clients and patients for your business or practice.

In this book, we will explore some of the most common direct mail tactics you can use. We will go a little bit into the technical aspects of how to use them. The guidelines associated with each. And I will give you some insider tips and share some success stories in hopes that you will consider direct mail as a viable marketing tool for your business or practice.

Direct mail can be traced back to ancient Egypt (1000 B.C.) where an Egyptian landowner created an ad on papyrus paper soliciting the return of one of his runaway slaves. It wasn't until the invention of the modern printing press in the late 15th century that its use became more widespread. The first direct mail advertisement in the United States dates back to the early 1680's and is an ad for real estate.

With the advancements in technology direct mail has evolved and taken on a whole new dimension enticing people and businesses to visit a website, call a phone number or return pre-paid envelope or postcard. These are great strategies and should all be considered because they allow new leads to interact with your business or practice.

And for those of you that believe that direct mail is dying or dead, I have an interesting fact for you. Did you know that according to Target Marketing Google, the online search engine, is consistently among the top 10 technology users of direct mail? That's right Google uses direct mail to generate new business for their Adwords programs. So if direct mail is good enough for Google isn't it good enough for your business or practice? Do you think Google could possibly have more resources available to them to research and determine that direct mail is a reliable and repeatable source of new customers, clients and patients? Could they have done just a little bit more research than you?

If you're like most business owners, you probably had a bad experience with direct mail in the past. A slick direct mail sales person or printer possibly convinced you to mail a large number of postcards with a weak message or offer to a poorly selected list that received little or no response because you had no tracking mechanism built in.

As I stated, you probably didn't even consider that maybe your offer was not good or that your list was terrible or that maybe the timing of the mailing was all wrong. Well if this was the case and you had no way to track the results of your campaign you would swear to people that direct mail does not work. Fortunately for you, this book is going to prove to you the complete opposite. And it's going to give you strategies and tips that you can use to get more new customers, clients and patients.

A question that I'm often asked is what is a typical response rate for a direct mail campaign? My answer that I've borrowed from one of my mentors the great Dane Jackson, of the "I Love Marketing" podcast, is that you can expect a response of between 0 and 100%.

Think about that for a second what am I telling you when I gave you that answer? What I'm saying is that the response of your mail out is really hard to pin down because it depends not only on when you mail your piece it also depends on who you're sending it to and what your offer is.

For instance, somebody who just bought a car wouldn't be interested in getting a direct mail piece from an auto dealership. On the other hand, somebody who's seriously considering braces for their son or daughter is a perfect candidate for a postcard from an orthodontist.

I will admit that response rate is, at a very high level, a good way to determine the success of a direct mail campaign. The best way, however, to judge the success of the same campaign is to use return on investment (ROI).

In chapter 7 we will talk about what return on investment is and why it's important to track. And in chapter 8 I'm actually going to give you some stealth tools, tips, and tricks that you can use to calculate the return of any direct mail campaign that you send out.

I hope this gave you a short and quick answer to the question, "What is direct mail?" In summary, it's a powerful lead generation tool you should be using to generate more new customers, clients and patients for your business or practice. If used in conjunction with other types of marketing and a strong follow-up program it could be all that your business or practice will need to get a steady stream of new customers, clients and patients.

2

POSTCARDS

The first direct mail option that I'm going to share with you is the tried and true postcard. I don't think there's anybody alive that has never received some sort of postcard marketing in the mail or at least seen one. They are very common and are one of the most basic things you can do in the direct mail world. It's a great starting point for a lot of businesses that are dipping their toe into the direct mail waters, but there are some things you should take into consideration.

On the technical side before you get neck deep in postcard marketing the first thing you should know is that there are dimensional requirements for a postcard in order for it to technically be considered a postcard by the US Postal Service.

The minimum dimensions a postcard must have is at least 3 ½ inches tall by 5 inches long, or wide. There's also a minimum thickness of .007 inches so a regular sheet of paper won't qualify you'll have to get something a little bit thicker. You're probably going to have to go with something like a 100lb uncoated text paper so don't just print a bunch of sheets of paper and cut them into fourths and think that'll do.

The maximum dimensions that a postcard shall not exceed are 4 ¼ inches tall by 6 inches long or wide. The maximum thickness is .016 inches thick which is about the thickness of 120lb cover or slightly thinner than light chipboard.

So those are the requirements that your postcard must meet in order for it to be considered a postcard and qualify for postcard postage pricing which is approximate $0.10 cheaper than full-service first-class mail.

Here's a quick tip you can use to figure out which side the Postal Service will consider the length and which will be the height of your postcard. Typically, on postcards, the length will be whichever is the longer side. The height would then be the side perpendicular to the length. ALWAYS put the delivery address parallel to the length on a postcard.

So while we're on the topic let's talk addressing. The delivery address is naturally one of the key components of a postcard and here are some guidelines that you should use when addressing your piece.

First, the delivery address and postage must always be on the same side of the postcard. This would seem like a no-brainer, but obviously, there are some people that do make this mistake from time to time.

Second, as I just mentioned earlier, the delivery address should be parallel to the longest side of the postcard. There's no need to beat a dead horse here, I hope you understand length and height, so we'll move on.

Third, I recommended that you ONLY use capital letters when addressing a postcard. The reason for this is that it'll make it easier for the USPS MERLIN™ tool to determine if your bulk mail meets the acceptance requirements. If the tool can't read your delivery addresses, you're not going to get a discount. Understood?

Fourth, use a font that's fairly easy to read. Specifically, no smaller than 10 point and I would recommend no larger than 24 points for all text. The Intelligent Mail® barcode, or IMb®, on the other hand, should ALWAYS be 16 point. Don't worry about IMb's at this point we'll cover them later.

Fifth, don't use any punctuation of any sort. For example, if you're going to abbreviate the word "Street" on the end of an address abbreviate it as "St" and leave out the period (.) at the end. This has to do with MERLIN acceptance, tip the odds in your favor and make it easy for the tool to pass your mailing. And you want the delivery address to be left justified the address and you want to make sure that there's one blank space between the city and the state and two spaces between the state and the zip code.

Finally, a key requirement for addressing a postcard is that you need to have a white background in the address section. So if your postcard is green or black for instance, you need to print the address onto a white background. You can print a white label of some sort or insert a white space into your piece that you're going to print the delivery address directly to. If you do not do this, your mailing will not qualify for bulk pricing because of address readability when it's analyzed by the MERLIN tool.

Ok, now that you're up to speed on addressing let's talk a little bit about postage requirements for postcards. As I previously mentioned, postage is typically $0.10 cheaper than first class mail. This includes full-service postage which means that the postcard will go out and a delivery attempt will be made. If the recipient has moved and there's a change of address or some sort of forwarding address, then the postcard will be forwarded to the recipient's new address. If there is no forwarding address or the postcard is undeliverable for any other reason, then a couple of different things would happen. The USPS would leave a notice for the recipient saying that there's a piece of mail at the post office that they need to come pick up or the postcard will be returned to you.

If you request an ancillary or additional service like "Return Service Requested" or "Forwarding Service Requested" on your postcard, then a couple of different things will happen. Most of them at no additional charge since you already paid for full service. Incidentally, you do have to let the USPS know that you want these ancillary services, you do this by printing the words directly onto your postcard somewhere above the mailing address.

If you request "Return Service" then undeliverable postcards will be returned to you with the recipient's new address or the reason for nondelivery at no charge.

If you request "Temp Return Service" then if the recipient files a temporary change of address, your postcard will be forwarded at no charge, but you won't be notified of the new address.

If you request "Address Service" then in the first year after the recipient moves, the postcard will be forwarded. You'll be given their new address and charged an address correction fee. In months 13-18, the postcard will be returned to you with the recipient's new address, at no charge. After 18 months, the postcard will be returned with the reason it couldn't be delivered, for no charge.

If you request "Change Service" then you'll be notified of the recipient's new address or the reason the postcard couldn't be delivered, and charged an address correction fee. Your postcard will then be discarded or recycled by the USPS.

If you request "Forwarding Service" then if the recipient has a change of address on file, the postcard will be forwarded for up to one year. In months 13-18, the postcard will be returned to you with the recipient's new address. After 18 months, your postcard will be returned to you with the reason it couldn't be delivered. All of this at no additional charge to you.

The postal service does offer you some pretty good ancillary services at little or no extra charge to help you keep your mailing list up to date and accurate when you pay full-service postage, I would recommend you take them up on the services if you want to keep all your information accurate.

At this point, you're probably thinking that what I've already shared with you is great information to have, but what you really want to know is where can you get a mailing list. Well, there are numerous mailing list vendors in the marketplace that can get you a mailing list. However, before we open that can of worms, I would encourage you not to overlook your own existing customer's list or "house" list.

If you're collecting customer information at the time of purchase, then you have a great place to start in the direct mail, with people that you know already like doing business with you. I would encourage you to test campaigns with your house list before you roll it out to a bought mailing list. If you get a good response from your "house" list, then chances are you're going to get a good response from a bought list. A good direct mail campaign is hard to keep down.

If you don't have a "house" list, then you're going to have to speak with a direct mail list broker. If you do a quick Google search, you'll find that there's multiple options in the United States and Canada. A broker can easily provide you a list of names that match whatever specific criteria or profile you're looking for.

One thing to keep in mind is that whenever you present any sort of direct mail piece to the post office for both mailing is that you WILL need to do some address messaging. This is a process called validating and presorting and is what allows you to qualify for the bulk mail rates.

In the case of direct mail postcards, there is no special rate classification for these pieces. You would fall into the same pricing category as letters. I'll dive a little deeper into this when it comes time to talk about letters, flats, and lumpy mail.

Something that I forgot to mention is that you don't necessarily need to have a return address on your postcard so if you don't want to include one it's OK, but I would strongly recommend you do so in case you would like to request any of the ancillary services the postal service offers.

I'm including a couple of different postcard examples so you can see the different concepts we introduced in this chapter. There are a couple of different size postcards that may or may not qualify for the postcard rate, but that are a postcard in nature.

This is one of our monthly lead generation postcards that we mailed as part of our "World Cup Fever" campaign. The size is 4"x6" and is printed in black & white directly onto colored card stock.

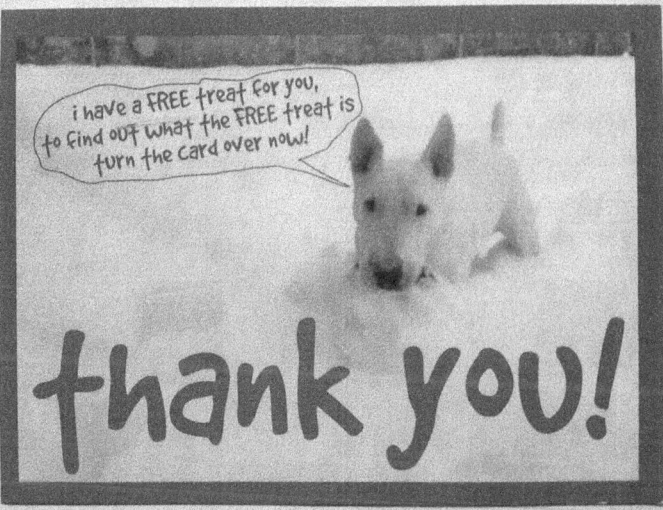

This is a "Thank You!" postcard we sent customers after they visited my store during the holiday shipping season. The dimensions are 4"x6" printed in full color onto some card stock.

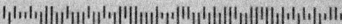

This is a postcard I received at my office from Staples®, it's 4"x5.25"
printed on heavy card stock, it also has a credit card shaped cut out.

This is another of our monthly lead generation postcards, the size (4.25"x11") exceeds the maximum postcards dimensions, however I'm sharing it because it's in postcard format.

3

LETTERS

The second option I would like to share with you is letters or sales letters as they are sometimes called. I'm sure we're all familiar with sales letters and I'm equally sure we've all received at least one in our lifetime.

Letters are very popular because they allow you to craft a longer message because you have more room when compared to a postcard. Postcards are great at grabbing a recipient's attention and it's almost guaranteed that it'll get seen and possibly red, but it does limit you as far as how much copy you can include on them because of their size.

A letter, on the other hand, allows you to include as much copy as you want by adding pages to your sales message and only for a fractional additional cost, so it's a great way to maximize your spend.

A challenge that letters do face so is that all mail is usually sorted over the trash can. The late great copywriter Gary Halbert said it best when he vocalized what many of us do without even a second thought. Sort our mail over an open trash can, discarding stuff that looks like junk mail and keeping stuff that looks like personal mail.

So a letter does have to capture a person's attention from the beginning and it has to compel them to open the letter and read it. Typically, what forces or compels, us to immediately open any type of the correspondence is anything that looks like a bill, anything that looks like it could be from the IRS or the government and anything that looks like it could be a letter from grandma.

What do all those things have in common? A couple of things but the biggest is that they don't have any unnecessary messages on the outside of them like, "Open me now!" or "Free subscription offer!" They are not necessarily in a bright colored or fancy envelopes. Often times the address is handwritten and they have a "live" Forever stamp in the upper right-hand corner so they don't look like junk mail. In other words, they look just like personal mail. If you're sending out a sales letter of any sort, it would be wise of you to keep this in mind. You do not want your letter to look like junk mail, so don't do anything that's going to raise any red flags.

So what are the requirements for something to be considered a letter? Well much like postcards there are physical requirements, both minimums and maximums. So for instance, the minimum dimensions of a letter are 3 ½ inches in height by 5 inches in length. The minimum thickness is .007 inches. Maximum dimensions are as follows, ¼ inch thick, which is actually pretty thick and if your mailing something thicker than that you're venturing into the land of flats or large envelopes which we'll talk about in the next chapter. The maximum height and length get a little bit tricky for letters, let me tell you why.

In order for something to stay within the maximum dimensions of a letter, it can't be any bigger than 108 inches in length and girth. Exactly! What the hell is girth? Great question and boy am I glad I'm here to tell you.

Girth is the number you get when you add the height and thickness of your letter and you multiply this number by two. To calculate the total length and girth of a letter, you would take the number you just calculated, the girth, and add the length to it. And if you remember from the last chapter the length is ALWAYS the side parallel to your delivery address.

Still not sure what the hell I'm talking about? Let me give you a quick example. Suppose you have a letter in a regular #10 envelope that's 9 ½ inches long by 4 1/8 inches tall and 0.05 inches thick. To calculate the girth, you would add 0.05 inches to 4 1/8 inches which gives you 4.175 inches. You then take this number, 4.175, and multiply it by 2 to get a total girth of 8.35 inches. But wait, the math lesson isn't done yet, take your calculator back out. You would then need to take the length, 9 ½ inches, and add your girth, or 8.35 inches, to get a total length and girth of 17.85 inches. Which is well under the maximum of 108 inches, any questions?

Now that math class is over you may be wondering if there any addressing requirements for letters? And much like postcards there is. Chief among them is that your delivery address has to be parallel to the length, or the long side, of your letter. So for instance, if your "carrier", which is another word for envelope, is 3 inches in height and 7 inches in length then you're going to want to address parallel to the 7-inch side. If you address it parallel to the 3-inch side then it won't qualify as a letter, so remember to always address it parallel to the longest side.

Also like postcards you don't need a return address so it's entirely up to you if you want to include one. If you're going to pay the bulk mail rate instead of the full-service first class rate, then you wouldn't be eligible for any of the ancillary "request" I talked about in the previous chapter unless you paid for them. So the use of a return address would be merely for strategic, get-my-letter-opened, purposes.

As far as the postage is concerned you have two options. The first option is to use a "live" first class stamp. As I previously state this will entitle you to all the ancillary "request" associated with first class mail. Which if you've forgotten are the automatic forwarding of the letter if there's a change of address and an address update postcard mailed to you so you can update your files. And undeliverable letters will be automatically returned to you along with a reason why the letter was undeliverable.

The second option is to pay the bulk mail rate. When you do this, you don't pay the full amount as a first class letter. You typically pay somewhere between 50-75% of the full amount depending on how your presorted ZIP codes break down. On its face it might not seem like a lot, but when you're mailing hundreds, if not thousands, of letters a year the savings can be significant.

To qualify for this bulk mail rate, there are a couple of things you need to do, though. Just like with postcards you need to validate and presort all the addresses on your mailing list. To perform address validation and presorting you need to run it through a piece of the software that updates all the dresses (validation) with the postal service's National Change Of Address database or NCOA as its sometimes called.

The way the NCOA database works is that when you submit you mailing list it automatically "crawls" trough all its change of address records and compares it with the addresses AND names on your list. If it finds a match then it substitutes your address with the address it has on file, it just assumes that it has the most up-to-date information. It's possible for there to be a match with no new address on file in the database as someone might've submitted a temporary change of address to the post office and never follow up by giving them a new address, thus no forwarding address. The software will tell you how many and which records were updated with a new address so you can update your records.

Another thing address validation will do is verify that the address is deliverable. What this means is that the address physically exists as a delivery point for the USPS. You may think that all addresses in the United States are deliverable, but this isn't the case. In some rural, and even some city, areas mail isn't delivered to a person's, or businesses', physical address. Mail might be delivered to a mail bank, a box at the post office or some other alternate location. When this happens, the USPS doesn't have a forwarding address on file for these deliveries because in their eyes these were never valid addresses. If this sounds strange, think of it this way. The address you have on file is a physical address NOT a mailing address, remember the two can be different.

The second thing you're going to have to do after validation is performed a presort on your mailing list. When you presort your list, you're sorting your letters and grouping them in like 3 or 5-digit ZIP code bundles. When you deliver your presorted letters to the Business

Mail Entry Unit (BMEU) they'll be in one tray, or sack, per bundle. Then all the BMEU has to do is run your letters trough their MERLIN tool and forward them on, in the same trays or sacks, you brought them into their corresponding post office's so a mail carrier can deliver them.

This is why you're getting that 50%-75% discounts from the post office because you're taking some of the work that they would normally do and doing it for them. It's worth repeating that the amount of your discount depends on your presort. The biggest discount is given when you can bundle your letters into like 5-digit ZIP codes (i.e. 79905 vs. just 799).

Two caveats worth mentioning here. One, in order to validate and presort a mailing list you will have to either work with a direct mail house or printer that can do this, so ask before you commit one because not all of them can. NOTE the USPS will NOT do any of this for you! If they did why would they give you the discount? And they usually don't like to recommend someone who does so don't call them up asking for this information.

Two, if you're going to be doing the validating and presorting of your own list you're going to have to buy a software license from a 3rd party vendor that has access the USPS NCOA database. The annual investment is significant and not recommend if you won't be mailing AT LEAST monthly. You can find a vendor online, they are all excellent and prices vary. There are also online services that will do this for you, but since I've never used them I can't speak to their level of service, accuracy or quality.

As an aside if you're going to be spending money to mail a postcard I would encourage you to possibly do a bulk direct mail letter because of the added room available to convey your sales message. After all, you wouldn't handicap your sales team by only allowing them to say 25 words to a prospective customer, client or patient before asking for the sale would you? Because remember direct mail is salesmanship in print!

For probably the same amount of money, you would spend mailing out a postcard you could get an entire multi-page letter because the savings in postage would offset any additional printing cost. So definitely, keep that in mind and remember that now that you do have the capability of conveying a longer sales message you have the challenge of getting prospects to open your letter. So there's a tradeoff, weigh if it's worth it for your business or practice.

What follows are a couple of different samples of direct mail letters. Notice the addressing. The style of envelope. How the different components are laid out. Overall letters are a great tool to communicate a longer sales message to your prospective customers, clients or patients.

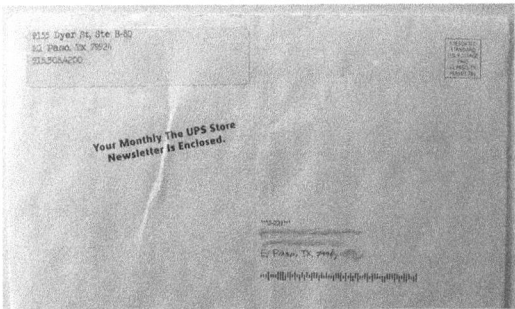

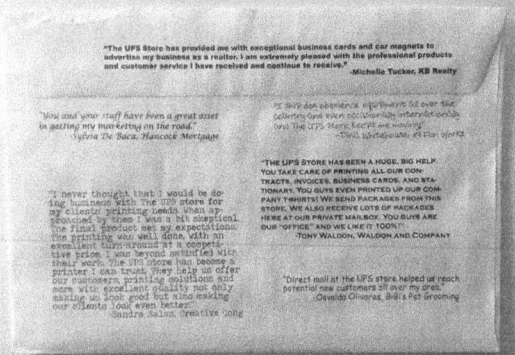

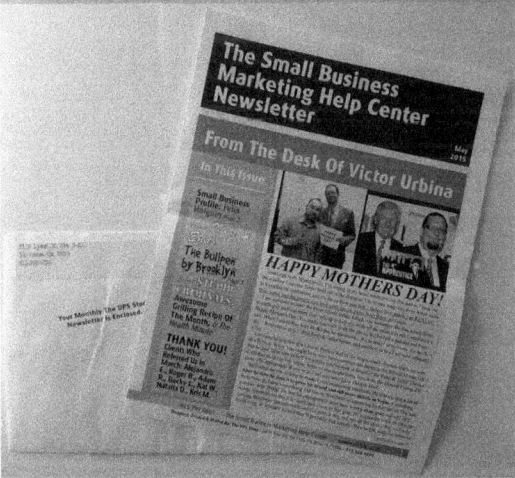

This is our monthly newsletter that we mail to customers & unconverted leads. It's a 6"x9" letter we mail using a pre-printed envelope that we print the address directly onto. We use a pre-printed indicia as well.

This is a direct mail package I received from **The Economist**. It's in a traditional #10 window envelope with a color logo, a pre-printed indicia and some teaser copy on the exterior. Notice they inserted an order form, business reply envelope and a brochure.

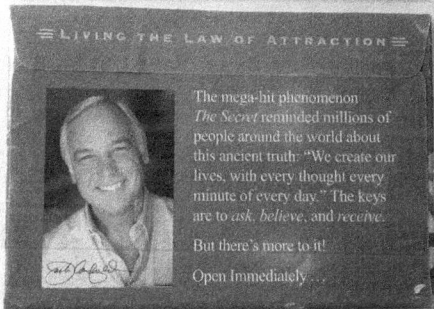

This is a direct mail package I received from Learning Strategies. It's in the previously mentioned 6"x9" envelope size except this version has a window and is printed in full color. The indicia is pre-printed onto the envelope along with teaser copy. They inserted 4 8.5"x11" pages.

4

FLATS

There is an option for you if what you want to mail is bigger than a standard letter size piece of direct mail or if you just simply want to make a bigger impact. The size that would come next is something called a flat or a large envelope and as the name says it's reserved for large and flat envelopes.

Flats are a great option for a direct mailer because not only do they allow you a longer sales message due to the additional real estate, but the simple fact that they are bigger and more obtrusive will command a recipient's attention when it gets pulled from a mailbox. I would encourage you to test a bigger size piece to determine if the increased cost to print and mail is justified with greater ROI.

Flat classification is reserved for large or oversized envelopes, but remember that in order for a direct mail piece to qualify as a letter it has to be no thicker than ¼ inch so it's possible for a small envelope that's thicker than a quarter of an inch to be considered a flat because of its thickness. I recommend that if your small piece is thicker than ¼ inch, you might as well consider enlarging the piece to the maximum dimensions a flat will tolerate. This will not only give you more room for your sales message, but it'll also, as mentioned previously, commands more attention at the mailbox.

The minimum dimensions for a flat are 6 inches in height and 11 ½ inches in length, which remember is always the dimension that's parallel to the delivery address. The minimum thickness is a ¼ inch.

The maximums are 12 inches in height and 15 inches in length. The maximum thickness is ¾ of an inch. These dimensions give you a vast array of height and length combinations for you to play with and determine what is the best dimension for your direct mail campaign.

As mentioned in the previous chapters there are addressing requirements for flat envelopes. The mailing address must be parallel to the longest side. A return address is not required and depends entirely on your campaign strategy and if you're going to be mailing at the bulk or first class rate. You should take this into consideration when you're planning your mail out.

It's worth repeating that if you're interested in having

undeliverable mail returned to you or if you'd like to receive change of address information directly from the post office for people on your mailing list then you will have to mail at the first class rate. Mailing at the bulk rate does not entitle you to these ancillary services because you're getting postage at a discount from the post office due to the fact that you're performing some of the work that they would do. However, you do forego these free ancillary "request" that are included in the first class rate.

There is an additional postage expense when you mail a flat. This is primarily due to the additional handling that will be required by the post office and is typically anywhere from $0.10 to $0.20 additional per piece, or on top of the letter book rate. Remember that the final rate is determined by your ZIP code break out after your presort is performed.

Mailing list for flat mail pieces is no different than for any other mail piece. There are numerous sources and list brokers available. As I stated with letters, whatever list you do wind up using, you will have to validate and presort your list before you mail. If you don't and you have too many instances where your mail out fails when inspected by the MERLIN tool, the USPS can revoke your direct mail permit. So it's best to always validate and presort properly and accurately.

What follows are some examples of flats, or oversized, direct mail pieces. Remember that a flat can be a postcard. It's the actual size of the piece that makes it a flat.

This is an oversized postcard that is mailed as a flat. It measures 8.5"x11" and has the mailing address printed onto the postcard after the larger postcard is printed. It also has a pre-printed indicia.

This is a direct mail package I received from Learning Strategies. The envelope is 11.75"x6" with a window and is printed in full color. The indicia is pre-printed onto the envelope and it has some exterior teaser copy. Notice the 5 inserted 8.5"x11" pieces in the envelope.

5

EVERY DOOR DIRECT MAIL

An exciting new entrant to the direct mail world is Every Door Direct Mail® (EDDM®) and, in my opinion, is a game changer for many businesses and professional practices. EDDM can be considered a hybrid of carrier route saturation. Don't worry about what carrier route saturation is, that's a very advanced topic for another day, another book.

What makes EDDM a hybrid is that it takes the existing carrier route saturation service and removes some of the requirements associated with it in order to make it more accessible to businesses and professional practices that aren't direct mail experts. The differences between EDDM and carrier route saturation are truly what make this type of direct mail so attractive.

The chief difference between the two is that you don't need a mailing list. In order to participate in EDDM, all you need to do is specify the carrier route(s) you want your pieces to be delivered on, that's it.

But where do you find the carrier routes? Excellent question! Carrier route information can be found at a great, easy-to-use website that was set up by the USPS, the address is eddm.usps.com. I won't go into all the details of how to use the website because there are already some great tutorials created by the postal service that can be found on the site, but make no mistake this is a great tool to use even if you're not going to be harnessing the full power of EDDM.

A second difference is that you must deliver your mail piece to every address along the carrier route meaning that you can't mail a partial route. Carrier route saturation does allow you a little more control here because you can leave out addresses from your mailing by simply removing them from your mailing list.

With EDDM, you don't address pieces to individual homes or businesses. Instead, you use a generic mailing address and the carrier knows to deliver them to every home or business on their route.

Naturally there are some minimum and maximum dimensions associated with EDDM and if they sound eerily familiar, it's because they are. The minimum height is 6 1/8 inches and the length is 10 ½ inches with a minimum thickness of ¼ of an inch. Are these starting to sound familiar?

The maximum dimensions are 12 inches high by 15 inches long and ¾ of an inch thick. Still not sure where you read this before? These dimensional requirements are almost identical to those of a flat!

There are some addressing differences between flats and EDDM though. When addressing an EDDM piece, the mailing address must be located entirely on the top half of the piece. The orientation really doesn't matter, whether it's parallel or not, as long as it's on the top half of the shortest side. If you're not sure what I mean, check out the illustration below provided by the USPS.

By far the most attractive feature of EDDM though, and what makes it a real game changer, is the price. When you use EDDM the discount you receive from the Postal Service is more than 80%, yep you read that correctly 80%, that's not a typo!

So what's the catch right? Why is the price so low? Well, the reason the price is so low is because you'll be performing almost 100% of the work. The only thing they'll have to do is deliver the damn things! And in case you've already forgotten you don't need to have a list, this is an additional savings of at least $100-$200.

The downside to all this, because there's always a downside, is that you're giving up control over what addresses you deliver to and that as of the writing of this book you still couldn't just deliver your piece to businesses along a route the way you can with residences. This makes EDDM a more ideal product for businesses and professional practices that have a mass general consumer appeal. Stealth direct mail insider tip to consider is that all businesses are med up of people who have to live somewhere, so I wouldn't automatically rule it out for strict business-to-business providers. In fact, your direct mail might work even better when you target a decision maker at their home where they might be receiving less mail, it's worth testing!

There are some additional bundling and paperwork requirements associated with EDDM. There is also a daily maximum number of pieces you can mail per business per post office. If you want to mail more than the daily maximum you can, but you'll need a bulk mail permit to do so. If you're not sure what that is, see Chapter 1 "What Is Direct Mail?"

EDDM is a fantastic option for businesses, and people (Lost your dog? Canvas your neighborhood with EDDM.), that don't have or want to mess around with a mailing list. It's great if you want to mail a big postcard or letter to people on a route because it's so much cheaper than everything else. Remember 80% OFF, that's like buying money at a HUGE discount!

As with the previous chapters, here's some EDDM

pieces for you to review. I've included three diferent sizes that all qualify for EDDM. Notice how much bigger they are than a standard postcard!

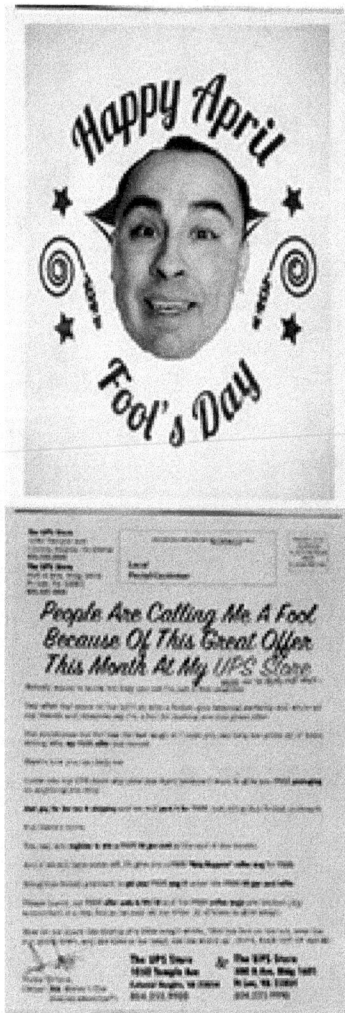

This EDDM piece is 6.25"x9" and printed on medium to heavy weight card stock. Notice that the address label and indicia are different from the other direct mail pieces. EDDM gives you more bang for your buck.

This is an alternate EDDM style, the piece is 4.5"x12" and it too is printed on medium to heavy weight card stock. This piece comfortably comes in beneath the maximum 15" dimension. Notice the address and indicia is printed on the top half of the piece.

This is EDDM style just barely sneaks in below the maximum allowable dimensions, the piece is 12"x15" and it too is printed on medium to heavy weight card stock. Notice the address and indicia are not in the same direction as the text, but they are place on the top half.

6

LUMPY MAIL

The final type of direct mail I want to share with you is dimensional mail, lumpy mail as I like to call it, or irregular mail as the USPS likes to call it. So what exactly constitutes lumpy mail? Well, as the names implies, it's a piece of mail that's not flat or that has three prominent dimensions that make it hard to miss or ignore, and many times peaks a recipient's curiosity.

Lumpy mail could be anything like a pen stuffed inside an envelope that makes it bulge up. It could be a mailing tube or an oddly shaped oversized bubble mailer. These are just two examples of pieces that can be classified as lumpy mail.

The objective of this type of mailing is to put something in an envelope, or container, that will create enough interest and curiosity by the recipient that it will compel them to open it immediately. Now I know that on the surface that sounds a little gimmicky, but I assure you that it's one of the most reliable methods of getting your sales message opened and read.

Of course you always want your lumpy mail to be directly related to your sales message whether it be directly or by using a theme to the mailing. For instance, if your business or practice is running a great limited offer you might include an oversized plastic clock in your carrier, envelope, along with a sales headline that reads, "You may not be aware that time is running out on this great offer so we thought we'd send you this clock."

Another example is you can send a miniature compass to customers, clients and patients you haven't seen in a while inviting back with a sales message that'll read, "We haven't seen you in a while so we figured you were lost, that's why we sent you this compass."

So yes, it can be a bit gimmicky, but it's less noticeable, and more appreciated when it's directly related to the theme of your mail piece or your offer. Of course you want to be sure that you're not tricking people into opening your mail with an unrelated product. For instance, if you're sending a plastic banana in your carrier and your sales message talks about coming in for a free facial and you don't connect the dots for people on why you included the banana then it's going to seem kind of random and inappropriate.

Incidentally here's a great way to connect the dots on that previous example, include a sales headline that says, "You must be bananas because we you're totally missing out on this great offer we have for you!"

Although it does take a little bit more time to execute, a lumpy direct mail piece is very profitable if you have the right offer, you're sending it to the right list and it's at the right time. You should always be on the lookout for anything that catches your eye that might make a good attention grabber because it'll look interesting inside of an envelope. All you have to do then is use a little creativity to figure out a way to incorporate it into your mailings.

Another popular mailing campaign is the "message in a bottle." For this mailing, you take a clear plastic water bottle and you stuff your sales message inside to create the message in a bottle. After you do this all you have to do is apply the mailing address, on a white label, and postage and the USPS WILL deliver this for you. Can you imagine what it would be like if you're the recipient of the message in a bottle? Think you'll be able to ignore it? Hell, you would even be able to bury it under other mail because the mail would just slide off, it would have to sit on top of everything else!

You can also get mail empty prescription pill containers, you know the kind you normally get from your pharmacy with your prescription label on it. Well what you would do here is similar to the "message in a bottle" campaign, you put your sales message inside and add the address label and postage and off it goes.

In cases where the product or service that is being sold is higher ticket I've seen businesses and professional practices ship, via courier which is still direct mail by-the-way, things as big as kayaks and paddles for a kayak. I've also seen full sized trash cans and traffic cones.

Your imagination is truly almost the only limiting factor to what you can direct mail. If the return on that investment is worth the expenditure, meaning the ROI makes sense, then I would encourage you to test it.

To use the USPS to fulfill your lumpy direct mail campaigns you're going to have to be aware of the dimensional minimums and maximums we had talked about in previous chapters. However, the maximum length and girth is what you'll have to always be aware of.

If you recall in Chapter 3, we brought up the idea of the combined length plus the girth to come up with the total allowable maximum dimension, for most direct mail pieces that would be 108 combined inches. A quick recap to calculate this dimension you add the length plus 2 times the height and the depth. If the dimension is below 108 inches, you're OK.

If, however, your lumpy mail exceeds 108 inches then there is a service called standard post whose dimensional maximum is a little bit higher at 130 inches combined length and girth. Yes, there will be an additional charge for this service, but it's definitely worth the additional investment when you're able to command your prospects attention and compel them to open your mailing.

The address requirements for lumpy mail are similar, but not quite as stringent as on other types of mail. It almost doesn't matter what direction you orient your mailing address label because the most important thing to remember is that it has to be on a white background. Most of the time what winds up happening if you're mailing something that's odd shaped like a "message in a bottle" is that they are processed by hand at the post office.

When you print your mailing address make sure that it's legible, meaning at least 10-point font, and in an easy to read font type. Please don't use extra or additional punctuation or weird abbreviations. If you're not sure how to abbreviate Avenue or anything like that, it's always best to spell out the whole word.

Postage requirements vary depending on the size of the piece you're going to mail, and you really have to pay close attention to that all-important length and girth calculation. Remember if you do go over 108 inches of combined length and girth, you will be required to pay an additional oversized fee. However, if the numbers make sense, you shouldn't let this stop you from doing this type of a mailing.

Normally postage on these types of mailings include the ancillary services like the return of undeliverable pieces and a postcard from the USPS alerting you of any change of address information for a recipient. For this reason, including a return address would be a good idea. I recommend that even if it's not included in the base price of your mailing, you should go and pay for this so that you don't keep people on your mailing list that have moved or no longer have a deliverable address.

Mailing list information can be purchased or rented from any list broker, and there should be no additional charge because you'll be mailing lumpy mail. You will have to validate and presort your mailing list beforehand if you're going to paying the bulk rate.

There is also some additional requirements and paperwork that you'll need to fill out for pieces that are lumpy or irregular. This varies on a case-by-case basis so it's my recommendation to reach out to your local BMEU and have a chat with him about what you're trying up mail. You want to ask them for the proper steps you would need to follow and the correct paperwork you would need to fill out in order for them to accept your mailing. The rule-of-thumb to follow here is that there is no rule-of-thumb, contact your BMEU and follow their instructions accordingly down to the letter. If possible, go down there with a sample of what it's you're trying to mail because an actual piece will do a better job than any description you could possibly give them.

What follows are a couple of examples of some of the really interesting pieces that I found and that are being used.

This piece isn't lumpy, but qualifies as a "grabber" its "envelope". Yes, that's a real Ziploc® sandwich bag. It's 6.5"x5.875" and is flat size, but due it being non-machinable requires additional postage. Notice the address is printed onto a white background and the "live" stamp.

This is a regular 6"x9" envelope that's been turned into a piece of lumpy mail by inserting a pen and a sheet of bubble wrap. They used a pre-printed indicia and printed the address in a faux handwritten font in black ink. This pieces definitely got beat up during its journey.

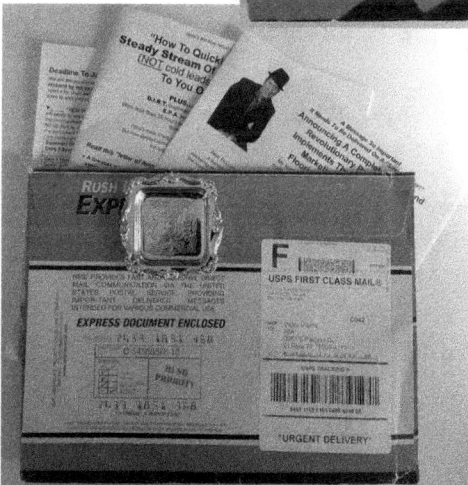

This piece is intended to simulate a priority envelope to create urgency, but they don't stop there. They inserted a plastic silver tray to make it lumpy. The piece is 12"x9" and doesn't use a traditional address label or indicia, again this is done to simulate an urgent priority service.

7

RETURN ON INVESTMENT

Okay now that we've talked about 5 of the different types of direct mail that you can use for your business or professional practice to get more new customers, clients and patients I think it's important to have a conversation about ROI, Return On Investment.

As with anything that you do you always want to make sure that you're measuring how much revenue your marketing is generating because there's no point in continuing a campaign that's not at least coming close to paying for itself.

One way to consider a marketing campaign is as if it was just another employee on your payroll. To illustrate this let me give you an example. Suppose you hired a sales person full time to drive new customers, clients or patients to your business or practice. But the sales person decided to only work half the time or even worse a quarter of the time or less. Would you continue to pay them their full-time salary or even keep them employed? I don't think you would. Well, this is exactly how you have to think about your marketing.

Marketing is an extension of your team. It's salesmanship in print that allows you to clone yourself and go out there and speak to 1000 different potential new customers, clients or patients when you, on the other hand, would be physically limited to maybe 10-20 on a particularly productive day when you have no interruptions.

The best thing about direct mail is that it'll never show up to work unmotivated or hung over. It will never cut corners or trying new ways to sell because they, "have their own style!" It will never not feel like working and will always show up ready to sell 100% of the time. Whether or not you actually get the sale depends on your message, your list and when your direct mail goes out.

Return on investment is a very simple calculation. The way you calculate it is you take all the costs associated with fulfilling your direct mail piece like printing, postage, graphic design, (if you outsourced it), etc. If you want to get a really exact figure, then you can even include the time it took to prepare everything whether you or someone else in your business or practice did it.

Once you have all these costs, you add them up to get a grand total. You would then take the grand total and you would use it to divide the total revenue that's generated. For example, if you ran a campaign that cost you $1,000 to get out the door and it generates $2,000 in revenue well then you would have an ROI of 2 to 1. This means that for every dollar you invested in it, it generated two dollars in sales. Not a bad return huh? You doubled up!

A question that I'm often asked is what kind of response rate can I expect from my campaign? The best answer I can give you is one I'm borrowing from my mentor Dean Jackson, "Well it'll be anywhere between 0 to 100%." You see response rate doesn't matter if the revenue is less than the cost because in essence you just sold a product or provided a service at a loss. But to answer the question, response rate is determined by your message, your list and your time of mailing.

As I've said previously, you shouldn't get hung up on your response rate. The thing to measure and what you should aim to maximize is ROI. Let me tell you why by expanding on the previous example.

The mailing cost you $1,000 to get 1000 pieces out the door. The offer on the mailing was for something you're selling at $100,000 each. If you had ONLY ONE person buy, you would have an amazing 100 to 1 ROI, which I would consider a home run. But you would have a TERRIBLE response rate of 0.1%.

If on the other hand you had the same mailing cost and the same number of pieces, but your offer was for something that you're selling at $10 each and you had 1000 people buy, what would the numbers look like? Well, first of all, you'd have a 100% response rate, which is impossible even if you're literally giving money away for free. But more importantly, you'd have an ROI of 10 to 1, which is still amazing, but considering the two different scenarios which would you prefer? Even if the ROI was the same, would you rather deal with 1 customer, client or patient or 1000 of them? I think the choice is an easy one to make.

The lesson here is not to get hung up on response rates. Amateurs talk about response rates, pros talk about ROI. If you want to really get a pros attention like myself share your ROI, even the bad ones because there's lessons there too.

Incidentally, a lot of the time when you talk to direct mail vendors or vendors in any sort of media or marketing, they'll want to talk about response rates, or views and reach. But while all these things are great to have, and the more of them, the better, the most important thing is ROI. How much measurable revenue did campaign generate, because the last time I checked, I couldn't pay for anything with views or reach, I couldn't even pay the vendors.

WARNING: Run away from any vendor who says they can guarantee you a response rate or ROI because they are lying to you. If they knew these things they wouldn't be there talking to you, they'd be out there making money with them?

A rule of thumb that I like to use for your determining if a campaign is successful are ROI indicators. Here's how it works. If I run a campaign and it generates less than $0.50 for every dollar that I invested in it, it's in my lowest ROI level which I call "the red zone". I will immediately discontinue that campaign. I won't repeat it. I'll study it to see what could have possibly led to the poor results. I'll take it as a lesson learned of something not to repeat.

My second ROI level, or "the yellow zone", is when I get between $0.51 and $0.74 for every dollar spent then that's a campaign that I will analyze very deeply again to determine if there's one or two things that I can systematically change and retest. What I'm talking about here is changing one thing at a time, the headline for instance, and then repeating the mailing to see if it improves the ROI. Once I've determined if it does I'll change another thing, the offer, to see if it continues to improve ROI. I'm going to constantly tweak components of this mailing, one at a time until it's reached my next ROI level.

My highest ROI level, or "the green zone", is for

anything that generates an ROI greater than $0.75 or for every dollar spent on it. I'll continue to try and improve the ROI to max it out, but if I don't get around to it and want to focus on adding a second campaign the augment this one I will do that instead. It just depends on the lifetime value of the customer it's bringing in.

Some of the time I might take a small loss on the front end, or during customer acquisition, because I know the lifetime value of that customer. When the lifetime value is high, I like to think that I'm making a small investment in that customer at the beginning of our relationship.

So a now you know why ROI is so important and why it's what you should be using to measure anything that you do in your business or professional practice. It should be the measuring stick for everything from employee training to new pieces of equipment, to employ themselves. Are you maximizing the ROI of ALL your assets?

8

HOW TO TRACK ROI

So now that we've learned about return on investment I want to talk a little bit about how to track the ROI of a campaign. It's not good enough to know about ROI if you never put it into practice so what I'm going to share in this chapter will help you do that. There are a variety of ways to track the ROI of anything you do an indirect mail. Direct mail is a little bit easier to track than some of the other marketing tactics that are out there.

The first tactic you can use to track ROI is to use a unique phone number on each of your mailings. If your primary offer is to call for an appointment or request more information, then you definitely will need a unique phone number. If you're only using this phone number on a unique mailing, you'll be able to directly track the revenue generated by your campaign.

If you're going to be driving people online, you

should create a unique page on your website to capture the revenue and leads. The worse thing you can do in this case is send prospective customers, clients and patients to your regular site. Why? Because you'll have no idea how many people showed up from your mailing. If you have a unique page, you'll at least know how many hits you get.

If either of these options are impossible or too high tech, then you can use some of the traditional methods. Tactics I recommend include a unique coupon or coupon code that you're not using anywhere else. Be sure that the coupon or coupon code is unique and that you're not going to be using it anywhere else any time soon.

Even when companies know these tracking tactics one of the mistakes I still see them make is they don't train their staff to ask for the coupons, how you heard of them or any sort of indicator that will let you know how this customer, client or patient wound up at your businesses door. No matter what method of tracking you use it's important to train your employees to ask for this information whenever someone new shows up at your business or practice or is on the phone with someone from your team.

A stealth tracking technique that I like to use if I'm not able to use a unique phone number because it may not be practical to get a new phone number for every single campaign I'm going to run is the following.

You use your regular already-listed-everywhere phone number, but enhance it by instructing recipients of your direct mail who call your business or practice to ask to speak with a specific person on your team. Now this person doesn't necessarily have to be somebody that's actually on your team. It can be a code name that you use to identify respondents to your direct mail campaign.

So for example, when a person comes into your business or practice or calls you and asks for Mary everybody on your team knows there's no Mary on your team, but that this is a customer that's generated by your direct mail. You can then help this customer and say something like, "Well Mary is not available right now she is helping another customer, client or patient my name is Samantha is there something that I can help you with?" At that point, you'll know exactly where this customer originated and the offer they responded to. Samantha will then be able to take the customer's order or answer any question they may have. The best part is that in the eyes of the customer they know no different because they are still getting exactly what they wanted.

One thing that as of late has become more and more prominent, that I try to advise my clients against is their desire to exclusively drive people from a direct mail piece to a website to request more information or to place an order. What I've found trough years of testing is that people are more likely to respond to your mail piece if you include a phone number to request more information.

The request for information, however, has to be viewed by your prospective customer, client or patient as very low commitment, though. What I mean by low commitment is they have to be relatively convinced that if they call the number they're not going to be attacked by a tele-shark and they can remain anonymous.

A good tool to do this with is the free recorded message or some sort of additional information hotline or "eavesdrop" line that a prospective customer, client or patient can call to learn more about your specific offer before they actually walk into your business or call your practice.

You have to remember that a lot of people LOVE to buy, but hate being sold. So they may not feel comfortable speaking with somebody if there are in the early stages of the buying process. It would then behoove you to have an alternate method for them to respond to your direct mail that doesn't necessarily involve calling and speaking with somebody or coming into your business.

So why am I anti-drive-to-web? Well, the truth is I'm not, I'm, however, anti-drive-to-web-as-the-only-method-of-response. Why? Let me tell you why.

The reason I advise against using it as the exclusive method of response is that most of the time there will be a period of elapsed time from when a prospect gets your mail piece and they sit down in front of a computer. By that time a million other things could've happened to them and even if they were interested in your offer and planned on checking you out, life happened and they forgot. How many times have you forgotten something you thought about doing only a few minutes before? See what I'm talking about?

Even if you're trying to generate sales directly from your mail piece, I would still encourage you to have them call a number to place an order and speak with somebody on your team. Not only will it allow them to have any additional questions and answered that they may have to the time of placing an order, thus eliminating the changes of an online abandoned cart, but it will allow you to start cultivating a relationship with them. It will allow you to start wowing them with your great customer service and depth of knowledge you and your team possess.

The second, and bigger, reason why I advise against drive-to-web-as-the-only-method-of-response is to get them away from the web where all of your competitors are only a mouse click away. This isn't to say that a prospect can't hop on a computer when they're talking on the phone to you, but at this point, they are no longer comparing you to everyone else based solely on price. They've been exposed to your customer service and depth of knowledge so you have the upper hand over your competitors who are just a website at this point. Let me give you an example.

Let's say you're selling tennis rackets via direct mail and you're driving all your prospects to your online order form if they want to buy. When they reach your online order form to place an order, there's nothing to stop that prospect from hopping over to Amazon or TennisRackets.com and comparing prices. If it turns out that they can buy the same exact tennis racket from Amazon or TennisRackets.com for $10 cheaper and get free shipping what do you think is going to happen? They're probably going to buy from someone them because they haven't had a chance to experience your superior customer service and product knowledge so they bought exclusively on price.

If this is what you elect to do, then the only thing your direct mail campaigns will do is create awareness and desire for products or services that another online business will fulfill. Unless you're the cheapest game in town and your margins are razor thing, but that's not the best business model to have because someone call always come in and sell cheaper than you. So why drive your customers from your storefront or office to a big shopping mall where everybody else can potentially be selling the exact same product or service you're selling? Think about that for a minute.

When you drive people to a free recorded message or phone number to place an order or book an appointment you can control the sales process. You can turn it into a one-on-one conversation. You're able to answer any questions or doubts. In essence, you're seen as a trusted advisor instead of a pushy salesperson.

By following this process people will already be interested in your product or service by the time they call you, the only thing they're looking for now is to have their final questions answered and be reassured that they're making the a smart decision.

In review coupons are great way to track ROI and motivate buyers. You can include a coupon on your direct mail piece as long as it's unique. You can also use a unique phone number if possible. If that's not an option, you can use my stealth "ask for Mary" technique. If you must drive people online, use a unique web page on your site to track conversions. Or go super advanced and high tech and use a PURL, which I didn't talk about because they're so advanced, but you should definitely look into. These were just a few tips and tricks that you can use to track, and hopefully optimize, the ROI of your direct mail campaign.

9

CASE STUDIES (PART 1)

We're coming close to wrapping everything up and by now not only have you learned about ROI, but I've also given you some ideas on how you can track it on your direct mail campaigns or any other type of marketing campaign for your business or practice. What I want to share with you know are a couple of direct mail case studies that highlight just how big of an opportunity you have.

The first is a very special campaign that I've run in my business throughout the years. The average ROI for this campaign bounces between $1.80 and $2.35 for every dollar I invest in it. This campaign is a lost customer reactivation campaign.

Now a lost customer reactivation campaign is a fairly easy campaign to run if you have an existing "house" list. Remember that what I mean by "house" list is a list of customers, clients or patients that have done business with you in the past or that came into your business or practice for an initial consultation and then never returned. They either bought the first time or they didn't, but they wound up on your list somehow and now you want to reactivate them.

Well as I said this is a very easy campaign to execute because you already know that these customers, clients and patients are interested in what you have to offer. You know this because they either already did business with you or they went as far as to come into your business or practice for a consultation of some sort. In order for somebody to come into your business or practice for a face-to-face consultation their interest has to be very high. Now for one reason or another life happened and they forgot all about how happy you made them when they bought or consulted with you. Well if you were smart, and you had a lead capture system in place when he first came in you're going to be able to check back in with them and find out exactly what's going on and remind them about you.

A little-known fact is that the majority of the customers, clients and patients that you've lost over the years you haven't lost because they moved, died or because they found someone with a cheaper price. The reason you lost them is simply because they think that you don't care about them! Here's how you can salvage that relationship, though.

Chances are these customers, clients and patients feel a little bad about the fact that they haven't returned and they just don't know how to get over that awkwardness of walking back into your business or office. They feel as if they'll be walking into a crowded room and all eyes will be on them. So it's your responsibility as the business or practice owner to invite him back in. To take that first step to remove the awkwardness barrier that stands between you and them. I think it's similar to having an old friend that you haven't spoken to in a while and you been meaning to call them for a weeks or months and you just haven't gotten around to it. Before you know, it's been years since you spoke with them and you find it only gets hard to reach out to them because it's been so long.

Consider this analogy when you think about your lost customers. They might be going through the exact same thing. They may be trying to figure out how to come back to your business or practice. A lost customer reactivation campaign takes the pressure off of them and invites them back in.

The campaign that we run is a one-step direct mail letter that we send to our "house" list. The letter is written in my wife's voice and appears to be coming directly from her. The theme of the letter is a customer is getting this "secret" letter from her because she's noticed that I haven't been myself lately. In the letter, my wife goes on to explain to them that she's noticed my odd behavior and she knows that it's because I miss seeing them at my stores. My wife then goes on to invite them back into the store and entices them by including a coupon in the form of a "personal check" made out to them that they can "cash" at my store the next time they buy something.

The letter itself is about ¾ of a page long printed onto yellow legal pad paper. We mail it in a plain white #10 envelope with a direct mail indicia, meaning we pay the bulk rate because we don't use a "live" stamp. We do include the return address on the envelope but don't request any of the ancillary services since we have our own list validation software in-house to update any address and run a presort before we mail.

We've been successfully running this campaign for about 3 years now and every time we break it back out the campaign returns right around $2 for every dollar we invest in it. The ROI would be higher if we sold a higher ticket item, but I'm very happy with this ROI so I'm not complaining, but imagine what it would do for your business or practice if your average sales were in the hundreds or thousands!

A comment we often hear from customers is that it was a good thing that they got that letter in the mail because they were actually thinking about doing business with us and for one reason or another they had forgotten or got delayed. Imagine that, customers happy to get "junk" mail from us… that could be you too!

We mail this campaign two times a year. Once during the dog days of summer and once during our busiest time of the year when our customer counts are almost double what they are the rest of the year. Typically, the customers who respond to this mailing spend 35% to 65% more per transaction than our customers who aren't lost.

If you think you want to try something similar, but don't feel comfortable using your wife or your family in the campaign then you can use your office manager or one of your employees. You can have them say you've been irritable and stomping around the business or office the last couple of months and they know it's because you haven't seen them in a while. They ask for the customers help calming you down and invite them back in. To show their appreciation, they're offering the customer, client or patient a special discount. The key word in any these types of mailings is INVITE. You want to make sure you use that word because it will make a customer feel welcome when they do come back in.

Don't think that just because you're a professional practice you can't use this campaign because it actually works great. It'll work in any industry and in any market, so please don't immediately discount it. If you have any doubts whatsoever, take a small portion of your "house" list and test it to see what kind of ROI you get. Because as another mentor of mine Dan Kennedy likes to say, "If you follow industry norms, you get normal results!" If you want your business or practice to excel, you have to borrow things from OUTSIDE your industry.

The second campaign that we use with tremendous success is a newsletter campaign that we've also been mailing for about 3 years. The ROI on our newsletter has been phenomenal from the very beginning. Let me share with you some numbers.

Within 6 months of us first mailing our newsletter we had reached an ROI of $30 for every $1 we invested in it. Now two years later the ROI has come down a little bit and currently sits at around a very enviable $20 per $1 invested. Now if these numbers don't get your blood pumping, I'm not sure what will. If you want to sign up to receive our FREE customer newsletter so you can add it to your "swipe" file go to www.sbmhc.com, but let me tell you a little bit more about our newsletters.

We mail our newsletter once a month to prospects and existing customers. It acts as a form of lead generation with prospective customers and as a nurture tool with our existing customers. Technically it's four printed full-color 8 ½"x11" pages. It gets mailed in a 6"x9" white envelope with a bit of teaser copy on the front, and customer testimonials on the back. We print our return address and bulk mail indicia directly onto the envelope.

The content of the newsletter is all informational, but not boring. It has one longer piece written by me that is marketing related. It also has some smaller editorials that are either business or consumer related about things I find interesting and cultivate from either The Wall Street Journal, The New York Times or one of the many journals and books I read every week. Naturally there is some fluff in there like Sudoku and a "Stupid Criminals Section". Overall I try to make it interesting and educational without being clinical.

Some businesses mail two slightly different versions of their newsletter. One for existing customers, clients and patients. The other for prospects. The difference between the two is that the newsletter going to prospects is a little bit more about pitching the business and its services, the other is more about nurturing the relationship. We choose to mail the same newsletter to both groups every month and we include an offer of some sort as an insert into the newsletter so it stands alone and doesn't make the newsletter come across as too salesy.

I would definitely recommend newsletters as a great method of not only getting more new customers, clients and patients; but also as a way of nurturing relationships with current buyers. Why? Well because newsletters allow you to express your personality and share your point of view and opinion. It gives prospects and your existing customers, client and patients insight into what you're like and hopefully bond with you over shared points of view and opinions.

If you're not sure where or how to start it doesn't

have to be that complicated. Take a standard 8 ½"x11" sheet of paper and create a simple two-page black and white newsletter, it doesn't have to be anything fancy. If you're not sure what to write about or how long it has to be, don't worry. On the top front, all you'll need is the title of your newsletter and your contact information. The rest of the space can be you writing about something that's going on in your business or in your life.

If you write about something that's going on in your life make sure you can tie it in with your business (i.e. a dentist's office) or the theme of your newsletter (i.e. dentistry). For instance, my newsletter is naturally about my businesses, but the overarching theme is about marketing, customer service and to a larger degree entrepreneurship and small business. For that reason, everything I write about is trough that lens. I connect the dots for the reader and tell them how it relates to one of those things, I don't make the them figure it out for themselves.

I try not to be too clinical or boring so I try to let my personality come through in my writing. What I've found is that when you lower your guard and open up and let them peek inside your life a little bit your customers, clients and patients are able to better relate to you. This creates a bond between you and them that'll make it hard for a competitor to break by offering them a lower price on your product or service. Remember, people buy from people the LIKE and TRUST!

The back side of your two-page newsletter can be something fun that engages your reader. Maybe a crossword puzzle, Sudoku or a recipe. You can also use a small section to profile one of your products and service, a member of your team OR even better one of your existing customers, clients or patients.

So you see, you've got your awesome new two-page newsletter completed. Wasn't that super easy?

If you're going to venture down the newsletter road you have to commit to it, you'll need to have some regularity. Every month or every two months at worse, although for maximum impact I suggest monthly it's what I do. Don't mail one month then skip the second-month mail in the third month then skip two months in a row. And always try to mail around the same time of the month, because believe it or not recipients WILL come to expect it.

Most of all be patient. Although I was able to get great results within the first six months of mailings, this is the exception and not the rule. Not everyone rushes into your business or practice when they first start getting your newsletter. In fact, there's people that have been receiving our newsletter for the past 3 years and have still not done business with us, but one day when they will. I'm not going to let $5-$10 per year (about what I cost to mail one newsletter to one prospect for one year) stand in the way of me and a new customer.

A hidden benefit of a newsletter that you may not have even considered is that it creates your own media platform you can use to promote anything you like. You don't have to worry about the internet, Facebook or the government suddenly changing and deciding they're going to regulate your content (it will happen one day, watch) because it's all yours. The only people you'll have to worry about keeping happy are your already happy readers.

10

CASE STUDIES (PART 2)

This chapter includes additional case study success stories of businesses using direct mail to get more customers, clients and patients. The stories come from people whose businesses are as varied as people are different. I hope that you can look beyond the differences to think, "How can I use direct mail in MY business or professional practice?"

Chrissy Borchardt is a marketing consultant and veteran direct mailer who works with a number of seminar companies that use direct mail almost extensively to put butts in seats. This is what she had to say about using direct mail.

As a student of direct mail marketing for over 20 years, I've discovered the two most important components to consider when designing and testing any direct mail piece are:

1. Getting the mail piece noticed and opened

(focusing on the outside carrier (outer envelope)/
presentation)
   2. Presenting a compelling message or offer inside

Yes.... both are infinite, so establishing a "control" to
test against is crucial when your main marketing vehicle
is direct mail. In our business, we rely heavily on direct
mail to fill up our annual events.

Recently, in an effort to increase our conversion rate
on our control package, I decided to simply test changing
the color of the carrier in one of our tests. My hypothesis
was simply this: if we could just get more people to open
our package, our conversion rate would increase. In this
case, changing the color of the outer envelope so it stood
out against every other piece of mail someone held over
his or her garbage can would give us a greater chance
the recipient would open it.

Our existing control carrier was 6"x 9" in size and
an off-white shade. We had a type set font for the return
address and the address block. I had always wanted to
test a black carrier (same size) with a metallic silver
handwriting font (so it looked more like a personalized
invitation). The black carrier and silver ink would cost
us an additional $0.10 per package in material and
production costs, but we moved forward anyway hoping
my hypothesis was right. The result?

Far better than I could have imagined...

From just that one variable change, we doubled our conversion rate in that particular test. Our control package had yielded us anywhere from a .6-.8% return in the past and held pretty steady. This new black carrier pushed us up to 1.2%. Needless to say, we performed a greater scale test shortly thereafter (larger quantity), and when the results yielded the same higher conversion rate, we established the black carrier as our new "control".

"Doberman" Dan Gallapoo is a world-renowned copywriter, consultant and serial entrepreneur who has used direct mail to grow multiple businesses to six digits and beyond. During a recent interview, he had to say about direct mail.

I've been online and using email since 96 and I love it, but I've never abandoned the "old school" stuff that I learned.

I've seen businesses exponentially boost their sales by just adding direct mail. Sending good old "snail mail" once a month with an offer.

It still works! And there's a lot of reasons that you should do that in addition to your email.

Osvaldo Olivares is a small business owner who owns two dog grooming and boarding locations in Texas. Although initially hesitant to try direct mail he found that it is a reliable marketing tool for his business to get more new customers.

At first, I wasn't sure I wanted to use EDDM because I didn't understand it. No one had ever explained how it worked to me, they just wanted to get my order and move on. Luckily, I found a partner that worked with me and sat down with me and explained the entire process.

Our first mailing we mailed close to 5000 pieces to four different EDDM routes near two of my new stores. Within one week we started noticing that the phone was ring a little more and a little more, but that wasn't even the best part.

By the end of the month, we had over 25 new grooming and boarding customers at each location. Which for a new small business is HUGE. The sales from these customers was also higher than what we were averaging with our other customers.

What surprised me the most was that we didn't even do anything fancy on our EDDM. It was information for the stores like address and phone number, list of services and a couple of coupons. It was really basic information, and it still got us new customers.

Since then we've been using EDDM to reach new customers all over my area. You really can't beat the return we're getting. Where else can you spend less than $1 per postcard and bring in close to $7? It isn't rocket science, it's SUPER EASY! I plan on continuing to use it to grow my business.

David Hunter is a real estate agent in Ohio who has been using direct mail to generate new listings. He's had success with a number of pieces and shared this one in particular because it's one of his favorites.

We did this REALLY small mailing to an area of about 600 homes with a new postcard I had designed. Now the postcard wasn't going to win any design awards and it was printed on my regular HP printer on cheap, thin card stock.

Well we mailed it out at a cost of about $310 and we couldn't believe the response we got. It was more than we ever expected!

We had 8 home owners respond putting the reponse rate at a tad below 1.5%. But that's not even the best part.

We got one listing out of the mailing that generated a commission worth almost $17,000. That's an ROI of $55 for every $1 we spent on it. WOW!

The added bonus what that the 8 other home owners that respond could one day turn into another $17,000 commission. All we have to do is stay in touch with them and be there when they're ready to list.

David's case study is exactly why I love direct mail and think it's a stealth method to get more new customers, clients and patients. If your list is good and your offer is attractive it will pull people out of the woodwork to do business with you.

The great secret behind direct mail is that it allows you to take a prospect that are interested but not ready to buy yet by the hand and walk them down the path to purchase whenever down the road that occurs. You do this while your competitors completely ignore them and fighting for the scraps of the people who are ready to buy now.

11

A VERY SPECIAL OFFER

I hope that this book has encouraged you to try direct mail as vehicle to get more new customers, clients and patients. If you understand how cluttered your "inbox" is getting, you'll agree that direct mail is a smart option.

In the last decade first class mail volume has dropped by almost 24 billion pieces per year. As a result, your mailbox has become less cluttered. Chances are you could be the only piece of mail in your category a prospect receives that week or even that whole month. On the contrary, email continues to increase and there's now over 48 billion received EVERY day in the US.

Unfortunately, there is no silver bullet and in order for direct mail to work for you, it'll probably take more than one try. So it's important to have realistic expectations and above all else remain committed to your direct mail plan.

To help you on your direct mail journey I want to offer you a **FREE Direct Mail Marketing Audit and 500 FREE postcards** as a <u>Thank You</u> for investing your time and money in this book.

The Direct Mail Audit is a multi-faceted examination designed to identify how you could use direct mail to get more new customers, clients and patients. A comprehensive "Report of Findings and Recommendations" is what it generates.

If you're new to direct mail, it helps you craft your message or offer. Drill down on your target mailing list. And determine when the best time to mail would be.

If you're already a direct mailer then it examines what you're currently doing or have previously done. It pours over your results and highlights overlooked opportunities.

The Direct Mail Audit has a real value over $997, and produces an actionable plan for generating revenue with direct mail. To claim your FREE audit go to

www.FreeDirectMailAudit.com

or call our free recorded line 24 hours a day 7 days a week at **(888) 305-4945 Extension 500**.

I cannot thank you enough for the trust you have placed in me. I wish you nothing but success as you continue on your entrepreneurial journey.

CLAIM YOUR COMPREHENSIVE

DIRECT MAIL MARKETING AUDIT & 500 FREE POSTCARDS

FROM
VICTOR URBINA
(A REAL VALUE OVER $997)
YOURS FREE!
AT

FreeDirectMailAudit.com

OR CALL OUR RECORDED LINE 24/7 AT
888.305.4945 Extension 500

Appendix A

FREQUENTLY ASKED QUESTIONS

What is the typical response rate of a direct mail campaign?

A typical response rate can be anywhere between 0 and 100% to use the words of my mentor Dean Jackson. What's more important is to measure is the return on investment (ROI) of the campaign. Let me tell you why.

You can have a campaign with a horrible response rate, only 1 sale, that will generate $1M in revenue. Or you can have the same campaign with a very high response rate, 1000 sales, that only generate $1,000 ($1 per sale) in revenue. The question then becomes, which would you prefer to deal with.

You can also have the same campaign that still generates $1M in revenue, but if in the first scenario the

$1M is generated by 10 customers and in the second scenario is generated by 1000 customer which of the two would you prefer? Would you rather deal with 10 customers or 1000 customers to arrive at the same revenue? Which group would you be able to more easily deliver a customized-hands-on-VIP-experience to, the group of 10 or the group of 1000 customers?

Don't consider response rate the be-all end-all of determining whether something was a success or not. More important is its ROI.

How do I calculate ROI?

To calculate ROI, you add up all costs associated with a direct mail campaign like printing, postage, graphic design and possibly the actual time it took to prepare everything if you did it in-house to get a grand total. You then take the grand total and use it to divide the total revenue generated by the campaign.

For example, if you ran a campaign that cost you $300 to get out the door and it generates $1,500 in revenue then you would have an ROI of 3 to 1, or $3 for every $1 invested.

How do I determine if I my ROI is good or not?

I personally use three different zones: "red" if below $0.50 for each dollar invested, abandon the campaign; "yellow" if between $0.51-$0.74, tweak one component at a time and retest after each tweak to see if ROI improves; and "green" if $0.75 or greater, continue to tweak and test if you like or move on to your next campaign.

I would recommend you modify my ROI ranges depending on the lifetime value of your customers, clients or patients and your average ticket. The higher your lifetime value, the more you can afford to invest upfront to get a new customer, client or patient.

What has the biggest impact on ROI?

ROI is influenced by 3 different things. Your message or offer, your list or who you're sending it to and your time of mailing. All the components are closely interrelated, however if I had to place slightly more weight on one of them it would be list selection.

It's possible to have a good ROI with a sub-par message or offer if you have the right highly responsive list. On the other hand, even the best sales message or offer in the world would be ineffective to customers, clients or patients that are just not interested in your product or services.

What's more effective email marketing or direct mail marketing?

The answer is it depends. It depends on the three ROI influencers: message or offer, list, and timing. It depends on your response tracking strategy. It even depends on your overall media mix. Having said that, I wouldn't discount using one exclusively over the other.

In my personal experience, direct mail has outperformed email marketing for various reasons.

First, people's "inbox" is becoming more saturated with marketing messages and spam. Currently, there are over 48 billion emails received EVERY day in the US. Try cutting through that clutter.

Second, there's a lot more room in people's physical mailbox. The amount of first-class mail has dropped by almost 24 billion pieces per year in the last decade. Making the odds high that you could be the only remodeler or plastic surgeon a prospect sees in their mailbox that month.

Finally, open rates for email can be marginal at best. If they don't open your email, then they can't read your message or offer. A recent study by Constant Contact® found that the highest open rates are for religious organizations at only 28%. The lowest were a little bit under 8% for fitness and nutritional services. What that means is that if you send out a hundred emails only anywhere from 8-29 of them will be opened. Compare this with direct mail where a 100% of it gets opened, or at least inspected before tossing, and you'll see why I'm a big fan of it.

I wouldn't however completely abandon an email

marketing strategy if it's working I would simply augment it by adding direct mail into the mix or vice versa. The more media channels you have, the more omnipresent you will be.

How accurate are the response rate claims made by some printers, direct mailers, and marketing vendors/consultants?

I would warn you to be VERY skeptical of any printer, direct mailer or marketing vendors and consultants. I've had nothing but bad results and wasted money in the past when dealing with people of this ilk... if only I knew then what I know now.

Remember, there is no such thing as a typical response rate and anybody that claims they can give you an answer to this question clearly does not know what they're talking about. But it shouldn't matter to you by this point, you're interested in ROI, not response rate.

How can I guarantee a successful direct mail campaign?

The truth is you will never be able to guarantee a winner. It would be illogical to step up to the plate on your first at bat ever and hit a home run. There are things however that you can do to hedge your bets and possibly get a single on your first time up. Here's just a quick rundown of what I would do.

One, get a clear understanding of who your target customer is, remember list plays the biggest role in determining success. You can't polish a turd or a bad list in this case.

Two, don't blow your entire campaign budget on one mailing. Test in increments of 1000 names or addresses. The response and ROI you see from testing 1000 at a time will allow you to either completely change course or scale if you have a winner. The process is slow but definitely worth it.

What are some key characteristics I should look for in a direct mail vendor to work with?

If you're considering working with a vendor look for one that understands the role they'll play in your business or professional practice. Ideally, you want someone who will be more than an order taker or a "yes" man, or women. You want a vendor who sees themselves as a partner who provides continued guidance and support after the sale.

A "Done For You" or "Done With You" program that allows them to carry out and execute all aspects of your mailing for you so you can focus on running your business or professional practice is possibly the best scenario.

Most importantly, they should take the time to understand your business and your numbers before charging ahead with any recommendation. This is a sign that they have a firm grasp on the role ROI plays in any business.

If I do partner with a vendor is it illogical to request a money back guarantee?

At this point in my career, I wouldn't consider anything illogical. However, you're going to have a hard time getting anyone to agree to this. There are too many variables that could go wrong with a mailing and as they say in the direct mail world, "the client always finds a way to screw it up."

Either way, I would definitely request one. If you don't ask you'll get a "no" 100% of the time right? You might be able to get a limited money back guarantee for everything but postage assuming you followed their instructions down to the letter.

Appendix B

DIRECT MAIL GLOSSARY

The following glossary is curtesy of the United States Postal Service.

Advance Deposit Account – A debit account into which a mailer deposits funds that are maintained by the USPS and from which postage is later deducted at the time of mailing. (Also called trust account.)

Automation–Compatible Mail – Mail that is prepared according to USPS standards so it can be scanned and processed by automated mail processing equipment such as a barcode sorter.

Balloon Price – A price charged for Priority Mail (for delivery to Zones 14) and Standard Post items that weigh less than 20 pounds but measure more than 84 inches but no more than 108 inches in combined length and girth.

Bulk Mail – The term is generally used to describe commercial mail. The term "bulk mail" refers to specific minimum quantities of mail that are prepared as a specific class of mail at reduced postage. For instance, First Class Mail requires a minimum of 500 pieces for each mailing Standard Mail requires 200 pieces or 50 pounds for each mailing. The term "bulk mail" is synonymous with commercial, business, or advertising mail.

Business Mail Entry Unit (BMEU) – The area of a postal facility where mailers present bulk and permit mail for acceptance. The BMEU includes dedicated platform space, office space, and a staging area on the workroom floor.

Carrier Route Mail – Mail sorted by carrier route. The mail requires no primary or secondary distribution. The term is a general descriptor of the available prices for this type of preparation, which includes carrier route Standard Mail, carrier route Periodicals, and carrier route Bound Printed Matter.

Commercial Base – A pricing category for Priority Mail Express and Priority Mail that is less than the single piece price paid at retail, and that requires specific postage payment methods other than postage stamps. Payment methods depend on the class of mail and may include Click-N-Ship, registered end users of USPS approved PC Postage providers, or customers using IBI postage meters that electronically transmit transactional data to the USPS.

Commercial Plus – A pricing category for Priority Mail Express and Priority Mail that is less than Commercial Base pricing, and that requires specific postage payment methods and annual volume requirements.

Destination Entry Discount – A postage discount for depositing mail at specific postal facilities (e.g., delivery unit or network distribution center) that are closer to the final destination of the mail.

Dimensional (Dim) Weighting – Postage price for Priority Mail packages, addressed to zones 58, that exceed one cubic foot (1,728 cubic inches) are charged postage based on the actual weight or the dimensional weight, whichever is greater.

Full Letter Tray – A tray filled at least 85% full with faced, upright pieces. Each tray must be physically filled to capacity before the filling of the next tray. A tray with less mail may be prepared only if less–than–full or overflow trays are permitted by the standards for the price claimed. (Also see less–than–full tray and overflow tray).

Indicia – Imprinted designation on mail that denotes postage payment (e.g., permit imprint).

Known Office of Publication – The business office

of a Periodicals publication that is in the city where the original entry for Periodicals mailing privileges is authorized.

Mailing Permit   Permission to mail at commercial (presorted) prices.

Meter Tape – A piece of adhesive paper that is fed through a postage meter and imprinted with postage. The meter tape is then applied to a mail piece (usually a large envelope or parcel that is too big to fit through the postage meter).

Network Distribution Center (NDC) – The NDC network consists of strategically located automated facilities that serve as centralized mail processing and transfer points for designated geographic areas, including Area Distribution Centers (ADCs), Sectional Center Facilities (SCFs), and auxiliary service facilities (ASFs).

Nonmachinable – First-Class Mail letters that are square, rigid or have one or more nonmachinable characteristics are subject to the nonmachinable surcharge. Standard Mail letters with nonmachinable characteristics are subject to nonmachinable prices. Parcel Select packages that cannot be sorted on mail processing equipment because of size or weight must be processed manually and are nonmachinable.

Oversized Price – Standard Post prices for pieces

exceeding 108 inches but not more than 130 inches in combined length and girth.

Permit Imprint – Printed indicia, instead of an adhesive postage stamp or meter stamp that shows postage prepayment by an authorized mailer.

Postage Meter – A device that can print one or more denominations of postage onto a mail piece or meter tape. It is available for lease only from designated manufacturers.

PC Postage – Approved third party vendor software that mailers can use to pay for and print their postage using a computer, printer, and internet connection.

Presort – The process by which a mailer prepares mail so that it is sorted to the finest extent required by the standards for the price claimed. Generally, presort is performed sequentially, from the lowest (finest) level to the highest level, to those destinations specified by standard and is completed at each level before the next level is prepared. Not all presort levels are applicable to all mailings.

Presorted First-Class Mail – A nonautomation category for a mailing that consists of at least 500 addressed mail pieces and is sorted and prepared according to USPS standards. This mail may bear a barcode.

Presorted Mail – A form of mail preparation, required to bypass certain postal operations, in which the mailer groups pieces in a mailing by ZIP Code or by carrier route or carrier walk sequence (or other USPS–recommended separation).

Presorted Prices – Prices which are lower than single piece prices. In exchange for this lower postage price, mailers must sort their mail into containers based on the ZIP Code destinations on the mail.

Sectional Center Facility (SCF) – A postal facility that serves as the processing and distribution center (P&DC) for Post Offices in a designated geographic area as defined by the first three digits of the ZIP Codes of those offices. Some SCFs serve more than one 3–digit ZIP Code range.

Single-Piece – The "retail" or "full" postage price available for individual pieces of Priority Mail Express, First-Class Mail, Priority Mail, and Package Services. Single-piece prices are higher than prices available for commercial.

Sort – To separate mail by a scheme or ZIP Code range; to separate and place mail into a carrier case; to distribute mail by piece, package, bundle, sack, or pouch. (Also see primary, secondary, and tertiary.)

Sortation – The distribution or separation of mail to

route it to its final delivery point.

USPS Tracking – Is an extra service that can be optionally purchased by mailers to have their mailpiece scanned at delivery. USPS Tracking is available for Priority Mail, First-Class Mail parcels, Standard Mail machinable or irregular parcels, Package Services, and Parcel Select packages. Extra services fees are in addition to postage.

Weighted Fee – The fee charged the sender for Standard Mail pieces endorsed "Address Service Requested" or "Forwarding Service Requested" that are returned as undeliverable. The fee equals the single-piece First-Class Mail price multiplied by a factor of 2.472, rounded to the next whole cent.

Zoned Price – A price structure for Priority Mail Express, Priority Mail (except Flat Rate products), Periodicals (except nonadvertising portion), and Package Services (Standard Post and Bound Printed Matter) pieces that is based on weight and distance traveled (or zones crossed).

About the Author

*"Life is a series of missed opportunities,
so go for yours."*
— *Victor Urbina*

Victor Urbina was born and raised in El Paso, Texas, and has lived there for the majority of his life. He has been an entrepreneur since childhood, starting his own soda stand in the heart of downtown El Paso at the age of 11 that he operated for three years. He attended The University of Texas at El Paso where he received a bachelor's degree in mechanical engineering.

He has worked for some of the biggest companies in their respective industries. He started his engineering career in the corporate world at Applied Materials in Silicon Valley and later changed industries by going to work for General Motors in Kansas City. While still at General Motors, he received a Master of Business Administration, also from The University of Texas at

El Paso, working and studying concurrently. His tenure in corporate America helped him realize that he was an entrepreneur at heart and provoked him to return to his roots.

Victor opened his first UPS Store franchise in 2006 at Fort Bliss Military Base in El Paso, and within four months the store was turning a monthly profit. By late 2008, he purchased his second store, also in El Paso, and quickly turned a struggling store into a profitable one by restructuring operations and increasing customer sales. In 2011, he began a national expansion and opened three stores over a period of 15 months. Those stores are located in: Albuquerque, New Mexico; Fort Lee Military Base in Virginia; and Colonial Heights, Virginia.

The lessons Victor has learned in business have come the hard way at times. Most notably, a few years ago, he was on the brink of losing all of his business. He quickly had to learn how to effectively market his businesses and so began what has now become a lifelong journey and one that brings him tremendous joy and challenge. Within sixteen months of undertaking this new challenge he was able to bring his businesses back onto better financial footing.

As result of his success he was asked by colleagues and other business owners to help them with their own business marketing. The lessons that he learned during his lean times are the ones he now shares with them.

Victor has always been fascinated with medicine and more specifically plastic surgery. It was because of this fascination that he realized that the cosmetic plastic surgery market was no different from his own retail background and that they could benefit from marketing their services more efficiently to have a better lifestyle and more autonomy.

Today, Victor and his wife, Georgialina, who holds a Ph.D. in immunology and is an associate research professor doing lymphoma research at The University of Texas at El Paso, live in El Paso, Texas along with their four dogs and four cats.

Victor is actively involved in the community where he serves on multiple boards including the Boys and Girls Club, Community En Acción, and the Hispanic Chamber of Commerce. He was a board member on the Marketing Advisory Council for The UPS Store where he helped direct the $25 million-plus annual marketing and advertising budget to optimize ROI for all UPS Store franchisees. He is also the founder of "Photo With Santa Palooza" a yearly Christmastime event that gives low-income families in the community an opportunity to take a photo with Santa in exchange for a canned good.

Victor is proud of his Hispanic heritage and Mexican roots, but above all else, Victor is proud to be an El Pasoan.

¡Vamos Raza!